Settler Life in Canada
HOMES

BY JOY KITA

CONTENT CONSULTANT
JOHN C. WALSH
CO-DIRECTOR OF THE CARLETON CENTRE FOR PUBLIC HISTORY
DEPARTMENT OF HISTORY
CARLETON UNIVERSITY

True North is published by Beech Street Books
27 Stewart Rd. Collingwood, ON Canada L9Y 4M7

www.beechstreetbooks.ca

Produced by Red Line Editorial

Photographs ©: Hal Beral/VWPics/AP Images, cover, 1; duncan1890/iStockphoto, 4–5; Christine Manning/Shutterstock Images, 6; Harriet Dobbs Cartwright/Library and Archives Canada/Acc. No. 1945-30-1, 8–9; Library and Archives Canada/PA-073668, 11; North Wind Picture Archives, 12–13; NativeStock/North Wind Picture Archives, 14, 15; Alexander Sviridov/Shutterstock Images, 16–17; Paul Fearn/Alamy, 18; Rick Orndorf, 21

Editor: Alyssa Krekelberg
Designer: Laura Polzin

Library and Archives Canada Cataloguing in Publication
Kita, Joy, author
        Homes / by Joy Kita ; content consultant, John C. Walsh,
co-director of the Carleton Centre for Public History, Department
of History, Carleton University.

(Settler life in Canada)
Includes bibliographical references and index.
Issued in print and electronic formats.
ISBN 978-1-77308-358-2 (hardcover).--ISBN 978-1-77308-388-9
(softcover).--ISBN 978-1-77308-418-3 (PDF).--ISBN 978-1-77308-448-0
(HTML)

        1. Pioneers--Dwellings--Canada--Juvenile literature.
2. Dwellings--Canada--History--18th century--Juvenile literature.
3. Dwellings--Canada--History--19th century--Juvenile literature.
4. Frontier and pioneer life--Canada--Juvenile literature.
I. Walsh, John C., 1969-, consultant II. Title.

GT228.K58 2018   j392.3'60971   C2018-902673-1
                                               C2018-902674-X

Printed in the United States of America
Mankato, MN
August 2018

TABLE OF CONTENTS

LOYALISTS AND LOG HOMES 4

CANADA GROWS AND PROSPERS 8

INDIGENOUS HOMES 12

INSIDE SETTLER HOMES 16

Hands-On Project 20

Glossary 22

To Learn More 23

Index/About the Author 24

Chapter One

LOYALISTS AND LOG HOMES

Groups of settlers moved to Canada in the 1700s. They built new homes. They created new lives for themselves. Canada's population grew after the American War of Independence (1775–1783). This was a conflict between the newly formed United States of America and Great Britain. Many people living in the United States who were loyal to Great Britain left. They were called **Loyalists**. Many of them settled in Canada. The British government offered them free land.

Most of Canada was wilderness. It was a **vast** land covered in thick, dense forest. In addition to those who settled in the Maritimes, thousands of Loyalists looking for new lives made their homes in Upper and Lower Canada. These areas are present-day Ontario and Quebec.

Families had to work together as they settled the land.

Settlers built sawmills across North America.

HOMES NEAR WATERWAYS

Many settlers built homes along the shores of the Great Lakes. Settling near water was important. **Waterways** made trading with and travelling to other settlements much easier. Water also powered settlers' **sawmills**. Logs went to sawmills, where workers would split them into lumber.

Loyalists first settled near the Saint Lawrence River, the Bay of Quinte near Kingston, and the Niagara Peninsula. Settlers used what the land provided them. The materials needed to build log homes were all around. It made sense to use the trees to construct their first shelters. Settlers knew that building something quickly to keep them warm, safe, and dry was important. Wealthier settlers could hire people to build homes for them. But most settlers did what they could themselves or with the help of friends.

LOG-HOME STRUCTURES

Settlers who came to Canada in the 1780s built homes along the Atlantic coast. The settlements in New Brunswick and Nova Scotia grew quickly, helped in part by earlier white settlement in these areas. Other settlers moved into Upper and Lower Canada.

In Upper Canada, the British government gave settlers land. The government told settlers they had to clear 2 hectares of land. They also had to build a house. This was a big commitment. Settlers could not do this alone. It was back-breaking work. They needed help from their neighbours. Trees covered much of the land. Before the settlers could build a house, they had to clear away all the trees. They did not have machines to help them. They had only basic equipment such as axes and saws. Settlers used oxen to help. These strong animals dragged the fallen logs into place.

The roof went on after the walls were in place. Any gaps between the logs on the roof were filled with moss. Then the moss was covered with clay. The moss and clay helped keep heat inside the house. The materials also helped keep bugs out.

Chapter Two

CANADA GROWS AND PROSPERS

In the early 1800s, towns such as Brockville and London in Upper Canada had many stone and brick houses. The building of stone houses occurred when the stone could be found easily. Settlers in Kingston and Ottawa built lots of limestone buildings. That's because the stone was already there.

In the 1830s, wood-frame and brick houses with stone **foundations** replaced the simple design of the log home. Foundations helped make the houses last longer. After new homes were built, the original log homes were sometimes used as sheds for storage. The New England–style house was popular in Upper and Lower Canada. This house style had two storeys. It had windows and a front porch. It was made from plank siding or bricks. It also had a shingled roof. The wealthiest settlers built

Some stone homes in Kingston were built along waterways.

houses with red-brick walls. They had sheet-metal roofs. This type of house was expensive to build.

SOD HOUSES IN THE WEST

Millions of people settled in the West between 1867 and 1914. The government wanted settlers to go to present-day Alberta, Manitoba, and Saskatchewan. Land in these areas was not the same as in Upper and Lower Canada. Instead of thick, dense forests, the land was flat. The government offered free land to immigrants from Europe. Thousands of people came from Ukraine, Romania, and Hungary. People also came from Upper Canada. These families transformed areas of the Prairies into cities.

SOD HOUSES AND RAIN

Sod houses absorbed rainwater. After a heavy rain, it would be damp inside sod houses for days afterward.

Some settlers built log homes because wood was available. Other settlers built **sod** houses for their first shelter. Sod homes could be built quickly and cheaply. The only things that cost money were the windows and door, but these were comforts not every settler had. Sod houses were made from grass and dirt. The dirt underneath the grass was held together by roots. The settlers broke up the ground and dug up long pieces of sod. The sod was cut into blocks up to 80 centimetres long and sometimes 10 centimetres deep. The sod blocks were placed together like bricks. These blocks formed the walls.

Sod houses are also called soddies.

Long, thin pieces of wood covered with sod or straw made up the roof. Sod
houses stayed warm in the winter and cool in the summer. Settler families living
in sod houses did not have to worry about fire destroying their homes. The sod
was fireproof. But sod houses were temporary. They only lasted a few years
before they collapsed.

Chapter Three

INDIGENOUS HOMES

Indigenous Peoples built their houses throughout Canada long before Europeans arrived. Indigenous Peoples used the land in a different way than the settlers. They **adapted** to their surroundings. Where they lived in Canada determined what their houses looked like.

LONGHOUSES

Near the Great Lakes in Upper Canada, the Haudenosaunee made longhouses. They farmed the land and built houses to be long-lasting. These homes were solid and large. They were built with great skill.

Longhouses were built using **saplings**. Haudenosaunee took saplings and stuck them into the ground where they wanted their house. Then they bent the saplings toward each other to

Haudenosaunee means "people of the longhouse."

SIZE OF A LONGHOUSE

The average longhouse was 18 metres long, 5 metres wide, and 4.5 metres high. Sometimes more than 20 families lived in a longhouse.

Beds in longhouses were built along the length of the building.

form a barrel-shaped frame. Sheets of bark peeled from trees were attached between the tree poles.

WIGWAMS

Indigenous Peoples such as the Mi'kmaq lived in **wigwams** in Lower Canada. Up to 12 people could live in a single wigwam. These houses used small tree poles like the longhouse. Tree poles were driven into the ground. They were tied together at the top. This made up the frame of the house. Animal skins were then wrapped around the frame. Animal skins also covered the door. The ground inside the wigwam was covered with tree branches and blankets.

Wigwams can also be covered with bark.

A **hearth** was built in the centre of the home. Smoke from the hearth escaped through a hole in the centre of the roof. Some Indigenous people did not stay in one area for long. They travelled to hunt. They would leave the frame of the wigwam behind. They took only the animal skins with them when they moved. When they returned to the area, they would reuse the frame.

Chapter Four

INSIDE SETTLER HOMES

A log house was a **modest** dwelling. Not much could be done to make it fancy. Settlers did what they could to turn their rough house into a home. Many settlers started off with a one- or two-room house. They would usually build onto their house when they could afford to. Homes built in big towns were usually larger. They had comfortable furniture inside. The size and luxuries of the home depended on the status and wealth of the settler family.

Some of the first log homes had dirt floors. Wooden floors were expensive. Sand was covered with hot water to create a hard-packed floor. Some houses had large timbers for a floor. Settlers painted their floors if they could. But they could only afford paint if they had money to spare.

Visitors to Black Creek Pioneer Village in Toronto can tour restored settler buildings.

What are the advantages and disadvantages of the types of homes the settlers had? Why did settlers build homes differently than Indigenous Peoples?

Some families in towns lived in comfortable homes.

People living in log and sod houses could cover the openings to their homes with quilts. The quilts kept out the cold and animals. Few people had the tools needed to build a wooden door. Glass for windows could be bought, but it was expensive. Most settlers had to wait to buy glass windows. They had to save their money.

Large families built log homes with higher walls than others. They used the extra attic space as a bedroom for the children. Furniture was made from wood.

Mattresses were stuffed with corn husks, tree boughs, and straw. They were laid on wooden slats or logs for beds. The sod house was as simple as a log house. Blankets were used to divide the rooms. Sometimes paper covered the dirt walls.

All types of settler homes could have cellars. Cellars were dug under the house. They were used to store food. A trap door on the floor led to the cellar. A cellar could be 2 metres deep and 3 metres wide.

FIREPLACES

The most important feature of many early settler homes was the fireplace. This was where the family gathered to stay warm. It was also where meals were made. The fireplace was the centre of all family activity. It was built with stones. It was large and open. Iron teakettles and griddles were useful to settler women. These hung on iron hooks over the fireplace. This was how food was cooked. Stoves were invented in the 1830s. Even then, not everyone could afford to own one.

Kitchens today have many tools. Toasters, electric and gas stoves, and microwave ovens make life more convenient. The settlers didn't have these modern-day luxuries. Their homes didn't have electricity or gas. Lighting a room was not done with the flick of a switch. The glowing light from burning logs in the fireplace provided settlers with light. They also used candles. Settlers worked hard to build lives for themselves in Canada. This began with choosing an area to live and clearing the land. Then they built many different types of homes.

HANDS-ON PROJECT

SETTLER LOG HOME

Design your own miniature log home. If you lived in settler times, how would you want your log home to look?

What you will need

- Graham crackers
- Thin pretzel sticks
- Frosting
- Chex cereal
- Butter knife
- 1 plate

1. Take one graham cracker and cut one fourth of the cracker off. The one-fourth graham cracker piece that was cut off will be your door. It will not have pretzel pieces on it. Spread frosting on the larger graham cracker. Then, take a new graham cracker piece. Spread frosting on it.

2. Cut a new graham cracker in half. Spread frosting over the pieces. Cover all the frosted crackers with thin pretzel sticks.

3. Lay a new graham cracker down. Stand the frosted graham cracker pieces upright on the new cracker. Arrange them in a rectangle. Use frosting to make the crackers stick together. These are your walls. Next, place your door. Use frosting to make it stick to the crackers.

4. Carefully spread frosting along the top of your graham crackers.

5. Take two unbroken, rectangular graham crackers. These will be used for the roof. Carefully spread frosting across the crackers. Place Chex cereal pieces on top. Place the crackers on top of your walls. Arrange them at an angle facing inward. Use frosting to make the crackers stick together.

GLOSSARY

ADAPTED
to have become adjusted to something

FOUNDATIONS
structures that support a building
from underneath

HEARTH
the stone or brick floor of a fireplace

LOYALISTS
people who were loyal to Great Britain during
the American War of Independence

MODEST
limited or small

SAPLINGS
young trees

SAWMILLS
factories where logs are cut to make boards

SOD
land that is cut from grassland and contains dirt
and roots of grass

VAST
very large in size

WATERWAYS
bodies of water that can be used for travel

WIGWAMS
dome and cone-shaped homes built and used by
First Nations people

TO LEARN MORE

BOOKS

Hudak, Heather C. *Communities in British North America*. Collingwood, ON: Beech Street Books, 2018.

Hutchison, Patricia. *Iroquois Community*. Collingwood, ON: Beech Street Books, 2017.

Kalman, Bobbie. *My Community Long Ago*. St. Catharines, ON: Crabtree, 2011.

WEBSITES

CANADIAN MUSEUM OF HISTORY: FIRST PEOPLES OF CANADA
homes1.beechstreetbooks.ca

CANADIAN SETTLEMENT
homes2.beechstreetbooks.ca

PIONEER LIFE IN UPPER CANADA
homes3.beechstreetbooks.ca

INDEX

brick homes, 8, 10

foundations, 8

Great Britain, 4
Great Lakes, 6, 12

Haudenosaunee, 12

Kingston, 6, 8

limestone, 8
log homes, 6–8, 10, 16, 18–19
longhouses, 12–14
Lower Canada, 4, 7–8, 10, 14
Loyalists, 4, 6

Maritimes, 4
Mi'kmaq, 14

New Brunswick, 7

Saint Lawrence River, 6
sawmills, 6
sod homes, 10–11, 18–19
stone homes, 8

Upper Canada, 4, 7–8, 10, 12

waterways, 6
wigwams, 14–15

ABOUT THE AUTHOR

Joy Kita is a proud Canadian citizen. She lives in Ontario and works as a freelance writer. She is married and has four children.